UNFORGIVENESS, GUILT, AND REGRETS

"SCARS OF THE PAST"

Audria Newton

Unforgiveness, Guilt, and Regrets "Scars of the Past"

Copyright © 2021 All Rights Reserved

Cover Design by Audria Newton

Published in the United States by Audria Newton

ISBN: 978-1-7372173-2-9

CONTENTS

Honor Due To

I give honor to my Lord and Savior, Christ Jesus, who is the head of my life for making this possible for me. Without Him, I would not be able to have the ability to minister and tell my story of things I have been through to help others overcome their past. For without God, I am nothing and can do nothing. I understand that my life is not my own, and it is an open book. I am honored to be able to allow my life to be a living testimony. All glory to the Highest God for blessing me with this gift. I cannot forget about all my supporters, whether you are friends, family, or strangers. You all mean so much to me, and I thank you all for the love shown.

A Feast to Your Knowledge

Brethren, I count not myself to have apprehended: but this one thing I do, forgetting those things which are behind, and reaching forth unto those things which are before, I press toward the mark for the prize of the high calling of God in Christ Jesus. **Philippians 3:13-14**

Many people go through life burdened with past issues. They hold on to things that people have done wrong to them. Sometimes things are hidden in our hearts that happened years, months, and weeks ago. Instead of letting go to move on, bitterness develops and causes anger towards those who have hurt us. We must focus on the things laid out before us rather than the things that are behind us. Forgiveness is the key to moving forward.

We ask God to forgive us for our sins and transgressions, but how can He forgive if we do not? **Matthew 6:14-16 For if ye forgive men their trespasses,**

your heavenly Father will also forgive you. But if ye forgive not men their trespasses, neither will your Father forgive your trespasses. Unforgiveness hinders us from moving forward. We must let go of the pain, move on, and forgive. Do not allow others to hold you back from your future and your blessings that God has waiting for you.

Introduction

And when ye stand praying, forgive, if ye have ought against any: that your Father also which is in heaven may forgive you your trespasses. **Mark 11:25**

Unforgiveness, guilt, and regrets are three main barriers that cause people not to move on in life. Depending on what others have done, some allow past situations to stop them from receiving the blessings of God. See, God has so much to offer us, but He cannot and will not give specific things to us until we get some things straight. The troubles that have us so unforgiving are the things we have to get straight. One thing God is big on is forgiveness.

Guilt and regrets create unforgiveness. It does not even have to be other individuals that bring us to hurt. Sometimes the mistakes we have made in our lives make us have an alt against ourselves. A lot of times, we can put ourselves in situations that are not meant for us. We meet people and accept them as friends and the whole while God may not want them to be a part of our lives. I know because I have done it occasionally.

I can remember God speaking to me or feeling uneasy about a person I was trying to connect with. I would ignore Him and later regretted it. It can happen to anyone who is unlearned or undiscerned. Many of my faults happened when I was young and naive. There is so much I could have avoided in my life had I listened to the voice of God.

For many years I was trapped and enslaved to unforgiveness, guilt, and regrets. I made so many mistakes in my life that brought me to shame. I was such a bitter person for a long time. As a little girl, I dealt with countless offenses. I was a girl who just wanted to be loved and to fit in. And trying to fit in caused me to be hurt repeatedly.

I grew up with scars of the past in my heart. Over the years, trying to be friends with folks and make people like me, all I kept receiving was disappointments. My heart had become damaged. After facing several experiences of being hurt by men, by family, by people I thought were my friends, and by others, I became numb to feeling angry that I would say I forgave but really, I just suppressed those feelings. In other words, I buried the anger in my heart.

Growing up, I did not understand what was going on with me. I never understood why I was mad on the inside until I became an adult. For a long time, God was calling me to righteousness, and I struggled with that as well. I ran from my call, and that contributed to a lot of my disappointments throughout life. But in the process of trying to live right, God made me evaluate my life. It was then when I realized that my anger started when I was a little girl.

How many times have people hurt us, which makes us furious? Let me rephrase that, how many times have we hurt others and asked for forgiveness? Do you see where I am going with this? Yes, we cry out numerously how people did us wrong. However, we have hurt others knowingly and unknowingly as well, especially God. I had to think about that. I had to make peace with people I have driven mad or upset. Never think it is crazy or strange how God would flip the script on you to make you evaluate yourself.

The most important person I ended up asking to forgive me besides God was myself. There was so much rage towards me because of the ungodly decisions I have made. One was struggling with the call of my life; I was ashamed of who I was. One day I told God there is no point in trying to live right when I keep failing Him. I rather live and go back in sin rather than living for Him and be a hypocrite. God said in *2 Peter 2:21: For it had been better for them not to have known the way of righteousness, than, after they have known it, to turn from the holy commandment delivered unto them.*

I always took heed to that scripture because I was afraid. Even though I was already in Christ and turned my back on Him, I just did not want to be lukewarm. I will not serve Him if I am going to be a hypocrite. But one thing for sure, it does not matter what you say; you cannot run from God. God does not force Himself on you, but He will capture your attention, especially when you are a chosen vessel. In this, I have learned to forgive and move forward to be useful in God. The realization came to mind that it is not about me; it is about Him and Him only.

And they overcame him by the blood of the Lamb, and by the word of their testimony; and they loved not their lives unto death. **Revelation 12:11**

Chapter 1

Scars of the Past

Remember ye not the former things, neither consider the things of old. **Isaiah 43:18**

The past has a way of scaring people's hearts. And those scars make folks sometimes do some things they do not want to do. Also, some may even say things that they do not mean. The issue of the heart flows out of the mouth quickly if you are not careful. I have said some mean things and downed others just because I was hurting.

Darkened by the past, I faced several challenges I should not have. Numbers of things I went through I could have avoided had I forgiven. Do any of these thoughts cross your mind? Scars of the past take root on the inside of us. The wounds develop into unforgiveness. Unforgiveness

3

has taught me that it is one of the ultimate sins that people latch on to the most. When you are a child of God, you cannot move on or get to that higher place in Him until you allow Him to heal those broken places and those opened wounds.

So, where did my anger and hurt began? Born in a family of ten, being child number five, I did not feel like I belonged in my family. I felt like an ugly duckling because I was not so outspoken as the rest of my siblings. I felt like that was why it was hard for me to make any friends at school or anywhere I went.

In school, I was teased and criticized by other kids. In first and second grades, I got bullied by a bigger girl I thought was a friend and my only friend. I did everything she wanted until my older sister put an end to it when she found out. Even as I got older, the clowning me continued mostly every day due to how I dressed and my hair. Also, the other kids knew that I was not at all talkative or outspoken. I would never stand up for myself. I went home every day, pretending like everything was ok, yet my heart was mad on the inside. The bullying caused hurt to turn into bitterness towards my family. I would snap on them and have an attitude with them for no reason. That lasted an exceptionally long time until I was grown. And that is when I was able to see what was going on in my life.

I gave my life to Christ one day and understood why I was so mean towards my family. God showed me I was hurting and angry from when I was a little girl. It did not stop there, though. Over the years, I would constantly get mistreated by people I loved. I made friends and would cling to people quickly. I tried to fit in or make them love me. Being someone that would say yes and hard to say no caused a lot of heartache and pain. People would take advantage of me because they knew I was easygoing. One day my pastor told me that I easily get attached to people, and she was right. I longed for love to fill a void that I had, but I never received it.

Falling in love with different men I knew did not love me helped cause me to grow a bitter heart. All I wanted was to be loved. I searched for love in all the wrong places, not comprehending I had that love all along from God. False love had me blind. I would love hard and give all myself to a man. I also would put them before God. God repeatedly told me to love Him more than a man and sell myself out to Him, but I did not want to let go. I thought I was missing out on something when the whole time I was missing out on the blessings of God. As a little girl, I did not receive love I wanted from my father, so I searched for it in men. There was still that little girl in me looking for unconditional love.

In 2010, I got married to a man who was not in Christ. Battling with serving God, trying to live right, and trying to please my husband, who was just my boyfriend at the time, I felt lost. I loved that man so much. He was a childhood crush. We dated our senior year in High School then broke up a few months after graduation. I still engaged in intercourse with him over the years without a relationship. Then later, I got pregnant with my firstborn.

I was with someone else at the time when I had gotten pregnant. And unexpectantly, the baby turned out to be my ex's baby. Before I found out the baby was my ex's, my boyfriend left me for another woman. I found out from one of my sisters that he was dating a woman who worked for the same company as us. I asked her about it, and she confirmed that they were dating, living together, and shared a child. I was furious. I never did get a chance to talk to him about it because I just figured there was no need since he lived with her. I knew he would lie about it, so I left it alone.

It was eight months after birth. I took a DNA test because the guy who cheated on me decided we needed to get a test to justify himself. To my surprise, the results came out not to be his baby. I thought it was his because I had intercourse with him around the time, my cycle did not come on. But it came on after I had sex with my ex. He called me and tried to fuss at me, asking me why I cheated on him. I made it clear to him that he had no right to confront me. He was cheating on me throughout our relationship and had a baby on the way. I began cheating months before finding out he was dating another woman on my job. I found some condoms in his drawer. He denied it, and so I said to myself, I can cheat too. I was faithful to him throughout our entire relationship until then. Once we got off the phone, I immediately contacted my ex and told him he was my child's father. After I told him, we made an appointment for a DNA test and the results came to be accurate for him being the father.

Some months later, we got back together. Then about one year later, we got married. I was tired of having sex with him out of wedlock, as I tried to live righteously, so I decided to leave. He did not want me to go, so he proposed. Deep down, I knew we were not ready to get married, and yet, I wanted to do things right by God. Ignoring my intuition, there we were, at the courthouse, exchanging vows. We went through so much together during our marriage. Some infidelity took place, and I retaliated with the same thing which eventually led to a divorce. I wanted him to feel how I felt. That did not make it right, but that is what hurt will do.

You may have heard a saying some time in your life, "hurt people, hurt other people."

Constant pain builds up in us when others repeatedly hurt us. Instead of moving on and letting go, we suppress our issues. When someone else upsets us, it makes it even more challenging to let go. I went through moments of saying, "I forgave," when really, I did not. I was battling with a spirit of anger. I would think about what others had done to me in the past, and that angry Spirit would grow stronger. I told myself I was letting go of the past, but it was not so. All I did was go through the motions.

Self-hatred took control of me for a long time. I was angry with myself for all the repeated mistakes I kept making. After a while, as I was trying to live for the Lord, I kept falling into the same sins. Spiritually I dealt with a lot. I was being like Jonah, in the Bible, running from my call. I loved God, but I was not ready to come to the end of myself. One minute I would be on fire for God; the next, I would not. Lukewarm was what I was being. Now, my heart was in the right place, desiring to do right; still, I was doing my own thing. Conforming to this world and doing my own thing had me in bondage.

I made so many terrible decisions with relationships and finances, not knowing how to save or budget money. I was left broken and in despair. For years, I battled with hating myself. I had so many regrets, continually telling myself, if I would have done this or done that, this would not have happened. The unforgiveness, guilt, and regrets just kept getting deeper into my heart and soul. I wanted to give up on life. I faced suicidal thoughts several times because I was tired of displeasing God and others who looked up to me, especially my kids. I often felt like I let my children down and failed as a mother because of what I took them through. I constantly wished I would have stayed with their father and made our marriage work. Since I did decide to divorce my husband, I went through moving from home to home. I was back and forth moving in with my parents, I could not keep a job, and the worse thing was, I was hopping from man to man. I especially did not want my daughter to see different men in and out of my life. I often pray that she will never follow in my footsteps with men.

I came from a family who relocated several times, and the cycle fell upon me. As kids, my dad had us living somewhere for a few months, then the next few months another location. After I became an adult, it was as if I was taking my kids through the same thing. Because of unwise choices with money and my unwillingness to work out my marriage issues, my kids went through so much with my unstable living situations. There has always been guilt, shame, and humiliation within for how I lived my life. I always prayed and asked God never to allow my unrighteousness to fall on my children: if anything, let me face the consequences. If I would have let go of Audria and the things I wanted to do, my life would have been better.

One of the hardest things we face in life is coming to the end of ourselves. This means that you put yourself out of the equation and allow God to take over. There are many sacrifices when living for God, and one requirement is letting Him have control and not you. As hard as it is to deny yourself, it is a must. If not, you will find yourself going in circles in life.

Let me expound a little on circles or cycles of life. Because of unforgiveness, I found myself going in circles. Cycles are something that you keep going through repeatedly. Now in searching for love for me, I dated men who were not good for me. It seemed as if I was attracting the wrong type because of my vulnerability. Some men can see when a woman is vulnerable and use it to get what they want.

I was very vulnerable and easygoing, and because of that, I attracted men who were fishing for weak women. And because I would fall for their scheme and manipulation, I constantly received nothing but hurt and disappointment. Even when I got with a good man, I expected him to treat me the same way as the no-good men. That caused me to push the good ones away.

The unforgiveness, guilt, and regrets was the cycle I went through. I did not know how to love or receive love when it was available. Finally, once I surrendered to God and allowed Him to give me the love I was seeking, the right man came along. Also, I had to give up unforgiveness. So, I say this to say; whatever it is, you may keep finding yourself going through over and over again, evaluate yourself, and give it over to God.

Chapter 2

The Darkest Place

Let all bitterness, wrath, anger, clamour, and evil speaking be put away from you, with all malice. **Ephesians 4:31**

Even though we were born in sin and all sin is darkness, we sometimes face moments that are darker than other times. A gloomy and dark day for me was the day I had a miscarriage. I became angry, bitter, and hatred penetrated my heart. That time of my life was the darkest one I ever faced. It was not because of the miscarriage I was in a dark place; I was depressed and angry with God.

After graduating from high school, I moved to Norcross (Atlanta), Georgia, with an older sister. I met a guy who seemed to be the sweetest, only to find out he was not suitable for me. You can say that he was a wolf in sheep's clothing. I made one of the worst mistakes of my life by getting pregnant by him.

The first few months of dating, he was everything I thought I wanted in a man. After a while, he changed. He became someone who I did not recognize. After finding out I was pregnant, I went to a prenatal appointment and found out I had an STD, and thankfully it was curable. I confronted him and asked him did he cheat on me. He denied it. He said he still talked to his ex-girlfriend, but they were just friends. I knew better, though.

Being young and naive, I chose to stay in the relationship because of the baby. After the situation of him cheating, things seemed fine. He acted as if he were so excited about the baby and I thought he would be a great father. But one day, he showed me how much he did not care when I really needed him the most by letting me walk to work every day.

My boyfriend purchased a new car. I worked about one mile from where I was living. There were days I would walk to work because I did not own any transportation. You would think he cared enough to make sure I had a ride. Instead, he loved his car so much that he worshiped it. He would not let me drive regardless of my being pregnant.

After a while, arguing began. He belittled me and threatened that he would take my baby from me. There was so much stress taking place in my life. I also worked eight hours along with walking to work. Surprisingly, one day he let me drive his car to get my license because I only had my learners. He kept calling, pretending to check on me when he had never done that before. It bothered me because he cared more about his car than me.

Later that day, I notice some spots of blood in my

undergarment. I called my doctor and scheduled an appointment. The appointment was some days away, so I went to the emergency room. The doctor said everything was ok, so I did not worry, but he prescribed that I rest.

On the day I went to my doctor's appointment, the nurse told me that she did not see a baby on the ultrasound. She then told me it was a miscarriage. I had to schedule an appointment for a D&C (Dilation and curettage). A D&C is a surgical procedure performed after a miscarriage. I could not believe it; I called my pastor at the time, and she prayed with me and said all is well. She told me that everything would be alright. Little did I know, things would turn for the worst.

A few days before going to the hospital, things were fine. I was not hurting or bleeding. The day came for me to get the D&C. I was not worried because I trusted god and knew that my baby was ok. I waited and waited. Finally, the doctor called me in the back. They checked me and said the same thing, "there is no baby," and I just had to allow the miscarriage to run its course. I was in a miscarriage state, but it was not fully complete. I told myself that it could not be because God said my baby is fine.

Still trusting God, I left and went into the waiting room to make a phone call to my pastor. I told her what the doctor said, and she said, trust God, the baby is there, so I said, ok. After I got off the phone with her, my sister called me to check on me. I told her what the doctor had said, and one of her co-workers wanted to speak to me; instead of encouraging me, she told me I could not go by faith because a friend of hers went through the same thing and lost her baby. Before I knew it, not recognizing that it was a seed planted by the devil, all my faith went out the window and doubt took over. I got up and went to the restroom, and suddenly, I started cramping so badly. I went to use the bathroom, and a glob of blood fell into the toilet. All I could do was cry and say, oh no, this cannot be happening. Blood began to drip down my leg. I cleaned myself up and went to my car. I tried to drive home, but cramps came back, and they were so unbearable to the point I could not drive at all. I pulled back into the parking lot and entered back into the hospital. Everyone was staring, trying to see what was going on because I was crying so hard. A nurse came to assist me and took me to the back. Once I got into the room, the Dr. came in. I explained to him what had happened. He then responded and said that the miscarriage had wholly taken place.

They set up to perform the D&C. Once they were done, I was unable to drive. My sister and my boyfriend came to pick me up. Thinking my boyfriend would comfort me and would have had a little more concern than he did; he just said everything happens for a reason. Do you want to try again? Looking at him with shock and frustration, I said no, we just lost our baby girl, and all you could think of is having another one, let's just go home.

Arriving home, my sister had made it home before me. I was upset, but to make things worse, she came to me and said, you lied, you did not want your baby, "you had an abortion." Looking so lost and confused, I said, what are you saying? She had spoken to our pastor and said that she had told her I did not want my child. Filled with more pain and hurt, I said that is not true, and I did not have an abortion. She also showed me a paper that said threatening abortion on my discharge papers, which meant vaginal bleeding in the first twenty weeks of pregnancy, appearing with abdominal cramps. I explained to her that it is just a term meaning threatening a miscarriage. She said, oh, ok, but the pastor said you still did not want your baby. I said nothing else and just went into my room and cried.

Trying to figure out why the pastor would say I did not want my baby when I did. That does not make sense. With all that had just happened, my heart began to harden, and I grew angry not only with myself but with God. I often questioned God why He took my baby away from me when I wanted my child. With all the anger and rage I had on the inside; my identity had left. I no longer recognized who I was. The worse place you could ever be in your life is to be angry with God. God owes us no explanation or nothing at all. But sometimes, because we go through things, we blame God and become bitter towards Him. I had to repent and ask Him for forgiveness and before that, I found myself depressed.

I fell into a depressed state along with being angry. Depression took hold of me for weeks until God spoke to me. He began healing my heart after I realized why my pastor said what she said. I then came into the knowledge of understanding that I did not want my baby. Now I did not say it with my mouth, but emotionally I was wrecked, just thinking of myself. I put my boyfriend first because I did not want to lose him. I have always been someone who wanted to have my children's father in the same household as my kids and me. Loneliness had me blind and not thinking clearly. Even though my boyfriend mistreated me, I still stayed in the relationship. Staying caused me to lose my baby. I put my feelings and emotions above the safety of my child, making me selfish.

My boyfriend verbally abused me, stressed me out,

and gave me STD, yet I stayed, knowing it was unhealthy for the baby. I cried so much after my miscarriage. Also, I was sorrowful for being angry with God. I asked God to forgive me. Even though I asked God for forgiveness, I was still a bit mad at myself. I regretted every day staying with that man, knowing he did not love or care for me. I knew one day I would have to move on and let go so I could heal, and God did just that.

Later, I ended my relationship with my boyfriend. God then spoke to me and told me to minister my story to other broken women who have been through the same thing. For anyone experiencing the mourn of a miscarriage, let go and let God mend your brokenness. You may not forget, but God has the power to heal.

Chapter 3

The Root of it All

Looking diligently lest any man fail of the grace of God;

lest any root of bitterness springing up trouble you, and

thereby many be defiled. **Hebrews 12:15**

You are who you are. There is no escaping who God predestined you to be. But to be that person, there are things you must let go of. There is always a root to things that have you bound. So, if you want to be free from something that has you angry or held captive, you must deal with the source of it. When you can get to your situation's root, you can be healed and free from it.

A root and source of some of the issues that had me enslaved for a long time was low self-esteem. Low self-esteem took control of my life. I did not feel beautiful.

I felt like an ugly duckling, feeling like an outcast. As mentioned before, as a little girl who was bullied for years in school and taken advantage of had me feeling unwanted. I had dark circles around the eyes, my hair would be in short ponytails, and the clothes I wore were not so appealing. Also, being rejected by boys had me feeling unwanted. No one knew my struggles or what I faced daily.

Beginning in fifth grade, my family moved to another city which was a small place. Of course, I was the new kid in school and did not make any friends but a few. One girl did try to bully me and fight me, who later became my best friend, but another girl stood up for me. I always appreciated her for that even to this day. Over time, I learned of my first crush, which was the guy I married when I became an adult. At the time, he was not interested in me. I know we were just kids, but being so young, you do not comprehend what being turned down is. All you know is someone does not like you, and it hurt sometimes. Over the years, I would have interest in a boy who did not like me. And as many times as I got rejected, my little heart was becoming damaged. All I wanted was to be loved. I would contemplate in my mind growing up "am I ugly or why no one liked me." Finally, in ninth grade, I dated the only guy who had a crush on me, only to find out he was cheating. My heart was crushed. He was my so-called first love, as people say, not realizing that God is my first love.

Time and years went by with experiencing different relationships. I struggled with low self-esteem until after I had gotten married. I would wear certain clothing types to look sexy, or I would fall for a man who said I was beautiful, not comprehending that it was manipulation. Even while I became an adult, knowledge began to sink in that I did not love myself. There was always a little girl crying out for love on the inside of me. My husband was very annoyed that low self-esteem had the best of me. He would fuss at me all the time about how men do not care for women with no confidence.

Many times, I downed myself. One day a small and sweet voice spoke to me and said, you are beautiful. I did not understand it. Then it spoke to me again and said, you are beautiful because I created you. After it spoke, I realized it was God speaking to me. From that day forth, I was free from low self-esteem. I saw myself differently, considering that I am the daughter of the king, which is God.

As women, we are one of God's most precious gifts. We should never wait on a man or anyone to tell us that we are beautiful because everything God creates is beautiful. Low self-esteem can be powerful and sometimes causes you to do things you should not. I have so many regrets about guys from my past who I wish I had never met or gave myself to. For so long, God was trying to get my attention and help me see that He is my first love and my husband. See, He wanted to do so much in me and through me before marriage, but being stubborn, I did not listen, even after my divorce. He has shown me that His love is far greater than any man.

I was searching for love in all the wrong places. The love I longed for was that father's love that I never received. I never had a relationship with my dad the way I wanted. I could never talk to him about anything or even receive a hug that made me feel like daddy's little girl. There was a void that had a hold on me that helped create low self-esteem inside me.

A void of feeling rejected and not receiving true love

took root in my heart. That vulnerable young girl who searched for love grew into bitterness, pain, and hurt. The little girl never left me even as an adult; she remained on the inside of me. Searching for love led me to be accessible and vulnerable to men. I easily fell in love and slept with men quickly. I jumped from relationship to relationship. The search for love was an addiction and hunger. All the while, God spoke to me telling me, that love I am looking for is from Him. Although I knew God loved me, it was hard for me to receive it due to rejection. I dealt with a spirit of rejection that had me feeling unwanted and hard to obtain real genuine love. Therefore, I resisted God's love because I was hurting and battling unforgiveness towards some men from my past, especially my father.

I had resentment towards my father. I know he loved my siblings and me, but he really was not a man who knew how to express his feelings. As kids, we went through so much that my heart would grow cold against him. My dad was not easy to get along with. Constantly, there would be an argument between him and me when I became of ages. It had gotten to the point where I did not even want to be around him.

I know I was not right to go against my dad and fuss with him, but I was so angry with him. I would also say things to him that I later regretted just because I was hurting. The Bible speaks about honoring your parents. But, when there is anger within, things are bound to from the heart in words. In the last argument we had, I told him I hate him. Even though I said it, I did not mean it. I just knew it would hurt him when I said it, even when he tried not to show it. I felt terrible about it, and I had to go back and apologize to him. Enough was enough. I grew tired of being angry, so I made up in my mind that I will forgive my father whether he accepted it or not.

One Sunday, while attending a church service, a woman was testifying about how she was dealing with unforgiveness. Then some other people got up and testified about the same thing. I knew I needed to testify as well because, by our testimonies, we are overcomers according to the word of God. At first, I hesitated, but then I finally got up and I began to testify on how I was angry with my dad. I said some things about how it created me into a woman who jumped from relationship to relationship because of the void of love I dealt with.

As I was testifying, I was unaware that my father was sitting in the audience. My pastor pointed him out. I still did not see him, but just knowing that he was there, I could not finish telling my testimony how I wanted. I did not want to hurt his feelings, but it was too late.

After the church service ended, I ran outside to see if my dad was ok. I explained to him that I needed to release all the anger and unforgiveness I had towards him. He said he was ok and that it was between God and me. Although he said he was ok, I can see in his eyes that he was bothered by it. Some weeks later, I had to go back and apologize to him because I did not wholly forgive him. I called both of my parents on the phone and began to tell them both how sorry I was for everything I put them through. My mom did not understand why I apologized to her. Sometimes you must get things right with others even when they do not feel like you did anything wrong. You know when you have wronged someone whether they know it or not. After I got it right with them, I had to give my testimony once again. That time, I was able to express and say everything that needed to be said. And that was the beginning of my healing process. My heart began to be made whole because I released that alt of unforgiveness towards my dad. It was the root of the hurt and pain I had been dealing with since a child. Carrying unforgiveness, guilt and regrets contributed to seeking false love. But I am grateful to have a God who is so loving and forgiving, who never gave up on me.

Chapter 4

Thou Made Whole

Confess your faults one to another, and pray one for another, that ye may be healed. The effectual fervent prayer of a righteous man availeth much. **James 5:16**

The day I let go of unforgiveness, was one of the best decisions I have ever made. It felt so good to release what had me bound for years. As I gave my testimony about my father, I also mentioned how I was bullied as a little girl, how I battled with low self-esteem and how the love I did not receive from my father caused me to search for love in all the wrong places. You see, even as I gave my testimony, some other lives were touched. You never know what others are going through until you give your testimony.

After giving my testimony, things changed between

my father and me. We began to get along more and have conversations more often. Then the most devastating thing happened, my father passed away from congestive heart failure. It was a tremendous shock to everyone. It hurt deeply when we lost him. Two days before he died, I had gone to his house, and things seemed fine. When I was leaving, he sat outside on a bench where he always sat. As I pulled out of the driveway, a strong feeling came over me. I heard the Holy Spirit say to tell my dad that I love him, but I brushed it off. I did not know that would be the last time I would see him. He went to the hospital the next day in the middle of the night and was there until morning. I was at work when I received a call from my baby sister. She was crying and said that dad had stopped breathing. He was going in and out with his breathing. Immediately I clocked out and rushed to the hospital.

When I made it to the hospital, I went into his room, and he was lying on the bed, hooked up to a ventilator. I broke down and cried. Just to see him lifeless and hooked up to the machine crushed my heart. I instantly began to think about the day before how I felt when I pulled out of the driveway, and I did not listen to the Holy Spirit. The Bible says in **1 Thessalonians 5:19** not to quench the Spirit. This means when we hear the Holy Spirit speaking to us, we should listen. We may have quenched the Spirit many times in our lives because we wanted to do what we wanted to do or even confuse it with just a thought from ourselves. And in the case of my dad, I did not heed to the Spirit when it told me to tell my father I love him. I felt horrible about it because I wish I would have told him while he was alive and well rather than on his death bed. But even then, I could not hold that against myself for the rest of my life.

Finally, after getting myself together, I walked over to his bedside and told him I loved him because he still could hear. Within an hour, the nurse came in to tell us that he was gone, that he could no longer breathe on his own. My mother had to decide to take him off the ventilator. I did not want to accept my father's passing away. Yet, I knew he would be with God.

I rejoiced that my dad was right with God, so he made it into heaven. And not only that, I was also at peace that I still had a chance to tell him that I loved him before he passed. Some part of me had regrets because I wanted to have an opportunity to prove to my dad that I could be a better daughter and be successful. I know my dad was not too proud of the bad decisions I made. God spoke to me even then and told me not to allow that to get the best of me. I cannot change what has happened; all I can change is now and be better for the future.

Although my father is no longer here, I am happy and blessed to know that things between us became right. Had I not forgiven him, I would still be grieving and dealing with unforgiveness now. Sometimes those old thoughts and old wounds try to come back, but I immediately cast them down. I am so grateful that God healed me and set me free. Without God, I could not face the different challenges I have encountered. Only it is Him who gives us the power to overcome unforgiveness, guilt, and regrets.

God had to heal me of many hurts I have faced yet reminded me of how sometimes I have even hurt others. So many times, we forget how we have wronged others. I must say that I pray that if anyone has any offenses against me, they will forgive me. All the wrong I have done in my life; I am not to judge anyone.

Holding on to offenses is easy but letting go is the hard part. But we must forgive if we want God to forgive us. Even though it is not easy to let go of hurt, God's plan for our lives cannot go forth unless we forgive. I had to learn to forgive and allow God to heal me. God took my experiences and turned them into good by helping others. I can share my encounters of different hurts to help heal others. I pray for healing for anyone who is holding on to hurt that is causing unforgiveness.

I believe everyone has had devastating experiences many times in their lives that left them with scars of the past. Some face worse situations than others, and others take certain conditions harder than others. We face problems such as bad relationships, being persecuted, and so on that form unforgiveness, guilt, and regrets in our hearts. Even though we deal with circumstances, we must forgive, let go, and

41

move on. Now that I am older, I realize that holding on to the past hinders my future. So, through sharing my experiences, I pray somebody can be healed. My advice to anyone is to let go and let God remove your hurt so you can move on and live a peaceful life.

A Prayer to Overcome Unforgiveness

Heavenly Father, you are so good. I humbly ask that You will help me to overcome anything that may be hidden in my heart that is not like you. Lord help me to release unforgiveness, guilt, and regrets out of my heart, or anything that may hinder me from moving forward in You. Lord, I purpose in my mind today that I am letting go of the past. I forgive anyone who I may have an alt against right now. Lord, I believe that You can take every unforgiveness from me. I thank You that it is done.

In Jesus Mighty Name I pray, Amen!

References

King James Bible. (n.d.). King James Bible

Other projects to be released this summer

An Open Book "Unashamed Testimonies"

Women of Confidence Poetic Book

Contact

Instagram: pressingtowardsthemark

Facebook: Audria Murphy-Newton

Gmail: anewtonmarketing@gmail.com